James Payn

The House on the Hill

Stories for Charlie and Alice

James Payn

The House on the Hill
Stories for Charlie and Alice

ISBN/EAN: 9783337004927

Printed in Europe, USA, Canada, Australia, Japan

Cover: Foto ©Thomas Meinert / pixelio.de

More available books at **www.hansebooks.com**

THE

HOUSE ON THE HILL;

or,

STORIES FOR CHARLIE AND ALICE.

BY THEIR MOTHER.

PHILADELPHIA:
SUNSHINE PUBLISHING COMPANY.
1886.

HOUSE ON THE HILL.

These simple stories were written as a Christmas Gift for two little children.

Many of the incidents had actually happened to themselves, or to their Parents.

The favor they have met with at our own Fireside, has led to the hope that they might also interest other Children. For, though the writer may never again *hear* the pleasant voice of childhood, she loves to *see* its brightness ; and would gladly think she had added a little to its pleasures.

S. E. H.

LLEWELLYN PARK, *Oct.* 31, 1886.

THE

HOUSE ON THE HILL.

THE CHILDREN THAT LIVE ON THE HILL.

ON the top of a Hill, by the side of a wood,
Live two little children — they are happy and
good ;
They live all alone, with their Father and
Mother,
And try to be happy, and " love one another."

They have plenty of Pets—many chickens and hens,
A cow and a calf, pigs and rabbits in pens ;

Two horses, besides, often take them to ride,
And an honest old dog runs along by their side.

Then they've two little kits, that we must not forget,
They love them much better than either dear pet ;
Brown Daisy is one named, the other Snow-drop—
O how they will scamper, and tumble and hop.

When Charlie and Alice come out for a play,
Very close by their side the two kittens will stay ;
When dinner is ready to the window they come,
And they patiently wait till the children are done.

Then they put up their paws, with a very loud *miew*,
Say, "We're waiting dear Master and Mistress for you."
So, sometimes they have milk, and sometimes they have
    meat,
But they always get something or other to eat.

6

One day these two kits were in a very sad plight,
For a big barking dog gave them both a great fright;
They put up their backs, and with "mew, fit, fit, fizee,"
They ran fast as they could to the top of a tree.

So the dog stood and barked at the foot of the tree,
But the kits did not mind, they were safe as could be,
Until Ann, from the kitchen, come with a big broom,
And *she* made the bad dog run away very soon.

And one night when dear Alice was running about,
And stopped by the window, in the dark to look out,
She saw a black face, and two bright shining eyes—
O quick to her Father little Alice now flies.

But it was only old Mink, a neighbor's black cat,
Who came down that evening to have a good chat
With the two little kits—and so hungry was he,
He hoped they'd invite him with them to take tea.

7

Of their Pets I have told you, but not of the plays
Of these little ones, through the long summer days ;
And how in the winter, when snow 's on the ground,
In fun and enjoyment they always abound.

Come up with me, then, to the House on the Hill,
By the side of the wood, and the clear sparkling rill ;
You shall see all their Pets, with their books and their
      flowers,
And spend with these children a few sunny hours.

OLD JIM AND THE FOX.

A True Story.

WHEN Daniel was a little boy, he had a nice little sister, three years older than he was; but she was not too old to play with him.

One day, after there had been a great snow-storm, and the wind had piled the snow up in great banks, against the high stone wall out by the old barn, Daniel and his little sister went out to the snow-drifts, to slide down and make a nice house in the snow.

They had a shovel to dig with, and when they had dug a little way into the bank, Grandpa's old black dog Jim came along.

9

He thought they were digging out a rabbit or a fox, and so he went to work too, digging and pawing the snow with his two fore-feet, and throwing it back, as if he really believed there was a fox in the bank.

Pretty soon he got in away out of sight, and the children could hear him smelling, to see if there was a fox there, and barking ever so loud.

After a while he came out, covered all over with snow and wet, and he shook himself, so that the wet, melted snow came into their faces, and made them run and laugh heartily.

They ran towards the house, and old Jim after them. He thought it was fine fun, and jumped upon them, and knocked them both down into the snow, and as it was on a steep hill-side, they both rolled over and over in the snow, with old Jim after them, till they rolled quite to the bottom of the hill.

They went right into some bushes, and out popped a big brown fox, with a great flat bushy tail.

10

He ran straight up the hill, towards the barn, and old Jim and the children went after him, as fast as ever they could go.

The fox ran faster than they, but old Jim kept close to him, barking as loud as he could, and this frightened the fox, so that he jumped right into the hole in the snow-bank that Jim and the children had dug. They ran to the barn and got a board, and put up against the hole so the fox could not get out.

Then they went to the house and called Dana, the hired man, to come and catch the fox.

After a good deal of digging he got him out, and killed him. Then he took off his nice soft skin, and went into the barn and stuffed the skin with hay, so that it looked just as if it was a real live fox.

The children kept the fox-skin for a long time, and used to play with it, and as often as they showed it to old Jim, he thought it was alive, and would dance around it, and bark like a good-fellow!

11

SANTA CLAUS' GIFT.

T was the first day of December, and Christmas would soon come. Santa Claus sat in his big arm chair, with his pipe in his mouth —thinking, thinking if he could not contrive some way to make the little children try very hard to be good, so that he could give them more presents this year than ever before.

At last he laid down his pipe, and took off his queer cap, and rubbed his head very hard. Then he said: "Ah, I have thought of a plan. I'll do as the President does—issue a Proclamation." So he called one of his little printers, who print the pretty little books which

10

Santa Claus gives to good children, and said to him: "Get a big sheet of cardboard, and print upon it these words, in the gayest colors and largest type you have:

PROCLAMATION.

SANTA CLAUS PROMISES TO ALL THE LITTLE CHILDREN WHO WILL TRY TO BE VERY GOOD FROM NOW UNTIL CHRISTMAS, A NEW AND BEAUTIFUL GIFT.

SANTA CLAUS' CAVE, *Dec. 1st.*

In a little while it was finished, and very gay it looked, with its bright border, and red and yellow and green letters.

Old Santa Claus took it in his hand, waved it in the air, and then jumped into his queer little sleigh, with its funny reindeer horses, and away he went, bounding over the frozen ground.

Now, the little printers had made a great many

copies of the Proclamation, and they were all in a bundle at the bottom of the sleigh. I cannot stop to tell you what Santa Claus did with them all. You know he can go wherever little children live. Some of them he left at the book-stores and toy-shops, but I must tell you of one that he hung on the Great Elm, on Boston Common.

The moon was shining very bright, when he jumped out of his sleigh, took a little hammer from the big pocket of his shaggy coat, and nailed it up where the little children could easily read it.

Then he gave a merry little laugh, and went whirling away as fast as he came.

Very early the next morning, people were stopping to read the Proclamation.

First, in the early dawn, would come shop-keepers, and the poor seamstress, hurrying along, and going across the Common to shorten the way.

Sometimes they would be in too great a hurry to

"THEY SOON SPIED THE PROCLAMATION FLUTTERING IN THE AIR."

HOUSE ON THE HILL.   Page 15.

notice anything—even the white, crisp grass, or the beautiful pond, with its thin covering of ice.

But by-and-by the children themselves began to come, to walk in the fresh morning air, and play among the old trees. You may be sure *they* soon spied the Proclamation fluttering in the air, and all ran to read it. They were all very much pleased, and stood around the old tree, talking and discussing the matter. There was quite a hubbub of little voices, and many merry peals of laughter.

Almost all of them said they meant to try and get the new Gift—all but one naughty boy, who "did not believe there was any such person as Santa Claus."

The children were quite provoked when they heard him say this, and some of the boys proposed pelting him with snow-balls, or rolling him into the pond, for daring to speak so disrespectfully of their kind old friend. They did, indeed, run after him, and drove him from the Common.

I do not know what became of him, but I am afraid he found nothing but pebble stones and nut-shells in his stocking *that* Christmas.

Now, it would take quite too long if I were to tell you about all these little folks—how some of them tried very hard to be good, and others forgot all about it in a little while. But I would like to tell you something about three of them—two little sisters and a brother. Their names were Paul, Emily and Jennie.

They had come to walk on the Common with Nurse, who drew Baby Willie in his little carriage.

Paul had his bow and arrow, which he kept pointing up into the trees, threatening to shoot the birds and squirrels, while little Jennie begged him not to do so, though Nurse told her she need not worry, "there was no danger of Master Paul hitting them."

At last his bright eyes spied the Proclamation. "Hush, girls," he said, "there's a splendid bird; I'll have him," and, before his sisters could stop him, his arrow went whizzing through the air, and right through the centre of the gay letters.

All ran to the tree—Paul very proud of his exploit.

"It is not a bird, only an advertisement; and it's against the law to put them upon the Common," said he, very much disappointed.

"Well, read it Paul," said Emily. "I'm sure I'm glad it's not a bird." So Paul read it aloud. "Now, that's good," said he, when he had finished. "Santa Claus is a jolly old fellow. But what does he mean? I suppose we must do something grand—something that will show."

"To be sure," said Emily. "Of course he means that. Now, if we were only big folks, there would be plenty of grand things we could do. You might save somebody's life, you know, and I—"

"Well, any way, I'll try," said Paul. "Perhaps I'll think of something."

"And so will I," said Emily. As for little Jennie,

17

she did not say anything; she thought if *great* things were to be done, it was of no use for her to try. She could only be what her Mother often called her—"a little sunbeam;" always willing to help others, always pleasant and cheerful. She hoped Santa Claus would not forget her, if she tried to be a kind and gentle little girl. As for Paul, he walked home in quite a brown study. He went to school, but he was more fond of play than of books and study. Above all, he hated writing; and such ugly looking marks as he made for letters! You would think a whole flock of hens and chickens had walked, with muddy feet, all over the paper. This was a great trouble to his Father, and he often talked to him about it, and tried to make him take more pains with his writing.

Now, Paul resolved he *would;* and he was a resolute little fellow. He was determined, before Christmas, he *would* learn to write, and write well, too.

As for Emily, she thought and thought what she

18

could do. She often heard ladies talk, when they came to visit her Mother, about the poor, and of woman's mission being to visit the sick and miserable.

Now, Miss Emily was quite a little woman, and she liked to sit in the parlor and listen to the conversation of older people, though she did not understand half she heard, better than to play with Jennie and the dolls.

Well, this wise little lady thought of a great many plans—one was to ask her Mother to let her fill a basket with food and clothes, and go round and distribute them among the poor people. But then she was sure her Mother would not let her go alone, in the dirty, dismal streets, where the poor people live; and she recollected reading the story of a little girl, who went without her parents knowing it, and what trouble she met. So she concluded to give up this plan, and think of something else.

Perhaps she might take care of the sick. How nice

to be a nurse in the hospital, and have the soldiers all so grateful, and everybody praising her, and saying she was like Florence Nightingale.

Then she remembered how, one day, her Mother asked her to take care of little Willie, who was sick, a little while. She did not find it pleasant, and was soon tired.

No, she must think of something pleasanter than waiting upon sick people. At last she remembered poor Mrs. Watson, whose husband was a soldier, and had been killed in the great battle of the Wilderness. She had four little children, and worked very hard to take care of them. Emily's Mother often gave them things—food and clothes. Ah! she would make those poor little children some clothes for a Christmas present.

She ran to ask leave of her Mother, who was much pleased that she should think of so kind and useful a plan, and gave her some pretty calico, and nice red and blue flannel, for frocks and sacks.

Well, a very busy little girl was Emily for the next

few weeks, and a very industrious boy was Paul. He wrote a long while every day, and though his fingers felt stiff, and his back ached, he would not give it up.

The boys wondered what had happened to Paul, that he did not play with them as he used to do. Indeed, Paul and Emily were just as busy as two such little folks could be; and, I am sorry to say, so busy that they forgot to be kind and obliging to others; and sometimes, indeed, were quite cross and unkind. Baby Willie did not put up his little hands to go to Paul, as he used to do, when he came home from school; and Jennie never asked Emily to play with her, and help her dress her dolls.

Alas! in trying to do some *great* good thing, they forgot the *little* good actions that ought to be performed every day.

But Christmas came at last. They were to have a Christmas Tree, and their Aunts and Cousins were coming to visit them. But the evening before, they

21

hung up their stockings by the fire-place in their Mother's room, as though they thought Santa Claus did sometimes give his presents to fathers and mothers, to hang on the Christmas Tree, yet they would rather he would put them in their stockings this time.

Emily had finished a nice little suit of clothes for each of the children, and brought them to her Mother, who praised them much, and promised to go with her the next day to Mrs. Watson.

Paul had brought his writing books, and a nice long page he had written besides, for his Father to see.

He was very much surprised, but very glad and happy, and praised Paul a great deal.

As for little Jennie, she had nothing to show. All these weeks she had been very busy — helping Paul and Emily,— taking care of Baby — her little feet running up-stairs and down-stairs, to bring things for the busy ones. She never complained or fretted, but went on her own pleasant way, without thinking of reward.

Very early Christmas morning, Paul came knocking at the door of his sisters' room — so early that only a little bit of grey dawn was peeping in at the windows, and the children looked like little shadows moving along the passage to their Mother's room.

Very softly they opened the door — very softly, for they did not wish to waken their Mother so early. They crept up to the fire-place. Yes, there were the stockings, stuffed full, and sticking out in all shapes; and over them hung a large bundle besides. One more look to be certain — and then what little feet could help dancing up and down; what little hands could refrain from clapping; what little voices could keep from shouting!

Certainly, Papa and Mamma could sleep no longer.

Then down on the floor, each with a stocking, they sat. First, Paul untied his large parcel. It was a beautiful writing desk, containing paper, pens, pencils, wafers, envelopes, sealing-wax and seals, even a

23

tiny wax candle and matches—everything that one could need to write or draw.

On the outside, in golden letters, was his name, and "A reward for learning to write."

Then, in the stocking, he found a beautiful book, a knife with many blades, a fine ball, and every corner, to the very toe, was stuffed with candies and goodies. Happy Paul! it was just what he wanted.

Emily's big parcel was examined next. It was a work-box, complete with every article needed by a little seamstress, from the tiny silver thimble, and set of shining scissors, to the rows of glittering needles. There were knitting needles, too, and crotchet, and on the cover her name, and "A Reward for Industry." In her stocking, too, was a book, and a pretty coral necklace and bracelets, and as many bon-bons as could be crowded into so small a space. Emily was as delighted with her work-box as Paul had been with his desk.

And now they all turned to little Jennie and her

stocking. First, there was a doll, for its pretty head was peeping above the top of the stocking—and a beautiful little lady it was, dressed in the latest style, with pretty blue eyes, and long ringlets, and rosy cheeks, and on her sleeve was pinned a paper, with, "My name is Grace," written upon it.

There, too, was a necklace and bracelets, like her sister's, and quite as many "goodies." But far down in the toe, they felt a paper. Jennie's little hand soon pulled it out. It was a letter to "Miss Jennie." Mamma read it for her: "Santa Claus to his little friend, and to her brother and sister, sends love. He hopes they are pleased with their presents. But if they will look in little Jennie's face, they will see *she* has the best gift of all.

"There is no present so beautiful as a sweet and gentle face. To have this, children must be *always* pleasant, good and kind."

A pretty little ring was in the letter, and on it were

written these words : " It is better to be good than to be great."

CHRISTMAS DAY.

Christmas Day — the happiest day in the year — the festival of the whole earth. To all it brings joy — to children unmixed delight. Yes, even to the poor and desolate ones, even to them it is *the* happiest ; for seldom is their prayer for aid unanswered upon that day ; and the dear Christ-Child remembers the little children, and does not forget that he was once a Child in this weary world, and so He pities and comforts the forlorn little ones.

It was a happy day to Paul, Emily and Jennie. Paul and Emily had a long talk with Mamma, after breakfast, and they both decided that Santa Claus was right, and resolved to try Jennie's plan, and not neglect *little duties.*

Afterwards they went with her to carry the garments

Emily had made, to Mrs. Watson. They found her in a neat little room, in the third story of a house, that stood in a close, crowded street, where many poor people lived. Some of them were miserably wretched, but many of them—most of those who did not visit the dirty grog-shops and saloons,—though poor, looked happy and comfortable, and had decorated their rooms with bits of evergreen, and brightened them up in honor of the Christmas Day.

Mrs. Watson was ironing a snowy muslin dress—so nice and clear, it looked just as if it might be going to a Christmas party. Her children were playing with bits of blocks, and some old toys that Jennie remembered very well as having once decorated her own nursery floor.

But their Mother's face was sad, and a tear sometimes fell upon the soft muslin, and dampened it. Quickly as the hot iron passed over it, the tear would disappear. Ah, we do not think how many tears are

27

hidden away in the folds of the rich and beautiful dresses we so often admire.

"How do you do, Mrs. Watson?" said Mamma. "We have come to wish you a merry Christmas, and Emily has brought the children a little gift—her own needle-work. But I am afraid you are not well."

"O yes, quite well, I thank you, ma'm. But I cannot help thinking of my poor man to-day. He always had a holiday Christmas; and they didn't come very often. So he used to say we must enjoy them the more. Them were happy days, ma'm." And here the poor woman quite broke down, and throwing her apron over her face, she sobbed aloud.

The children all felt like crying with her, and the tears came into Mamma's eyes; but Bridget, who came with them to bring the basket, thought it would never do to cry on Christmas Day. So she seized the oldest child, and began to pull off his old, thin clothes, and dress him in the new shoes and stockings, and pretty sack Emily had made. He looked half frightened, half pleased; but when Bridget buckled a shining black belt around him, and put a nice little cap on his head, he began to laugh and dance about. His Mother looked up to see what was the matter, and when she saw her little boy looking so nice, and Emily and Jennie dressing the little girls, while Bridget had the baby stretched out on her lap, his fat little legs just disappearing in some bright red stockings, she could not help smiling, and was soon her own cheerful self again.

Mamma spoke words of comfort to her of her brave soldier husband, who had died fighting for his country. He was a good man, and though she would never forget or cease to miss him, yet she might hope to meet him again in Heaven.

"And now we must go. Bridget shall bring you a basket by and by; so do not think about dinner. And I hope these little ones will be warm and comfortable for the rest of the winter."

" Oh, and indeed they will, ma'm ; and many thanks to you and to Miss Emily, for your great kindness. Sure, I ought not to complain when I have so many blessings."

They reached home just as a whole sleigh load of uncles, aunts and cousins, drove up to the door, and oh, such a welcome!—the kisses and hugs, the questions asked, the merry laughter and the chattering voices. If it had been any other day, I am afraid some of the older heads would have ached sadly in so much confusion. But who ever heard of talking and laughing giving one the headache on Christmas Day!

Merriment and fun, candy pulling and games, were the order of the day, until they all assembled around the long table, in the pleasant dining-room, for an early dinner.

And now I am afraid I cannot do justice to that dinner, but if you will just remember the nicest, pleasantest Christmas dinner you have ever had—it was just like *that*. The big turkey, the monstrous chicken pie, the round plum pudding, mince pies, and with the dessert a bottle of currant wine Grandma had sent — her own manufacture.

I must tell you about that wine. Grandma lived away far in the country, and all around her nice, old fashioned garden was a hedge of currant bushes. So, every fall she would send a big box to her little grandchildren, and when they opened it, there would be a bottle of currant wine, with a neat little label marked, "For Christmas," another "For New Year's," another "Paul's birthday," "Emily's birthday," and so on through all the holidays.

So they all drank Grandma's health in a tiny glass of currant wine. Some very witty toasts were given, too, and they were quite as much applauded as some very wise ones at the big dinners.

Then came tea. It was always served on holidays in a little china tea-set of Jennie's, and *she* had the honor of pouring it out, and very nicely she did it too. Papa said it was the best cup of tea he had drank for a long time. Presently, Emily and one of her young lady cousins were discovered balancing their teaspoons upon the edges of their cups, and carefully pouring tea, drop by drop, into them, counting every drop. They were so busy they did not notice all had stopped talking, and were watching them.

"What are you doing?" said Papa. The little misses blushed, and looked quite confused.

"I know," said Paul.

"Please don't tell, Paul," said Emily in a pleading voice. Paul felt strongly tempted to tease the little ladies, but wisely concluded it would not "be doing as he would be done by."

"Well, never mind," said Papa; "girls will have secrets. See, I will show you a trick with this empty bottle. Can I put a glass of water in it without drawing out the cork?" Some of the older ones shook their heads, while the children all declared it could not be done. Papa quickly turned the bottle up-side down, and poured the water into the deep cavity, or depression, in the bottom of the bottle. The water was *in* the bottle, and that was all Papa had agreed to do—*in* the bottle, not *within* it.

All were delighted with the bottle puzzle. "It is like Columbus and his egg," said Mamma; "but see, it is growing dark; it will soon be time to light our Christmas Tree. I wish we could have arranged some tableaux, or something of the kind, to pass away this hour."

"Oh," said Papa, "Paul and I have a secret. Come, Paul. Ladies and gentlemen, you are invited to come into the library in about five minutes, and listen to an original dialogue, called "*The March of Intellect.*"

So they disappeared, and at the end of the five minutes, all the party followed them, to find a very wise looking gentleman, sitting by the table in an arm-chair,

reading a big book, and little Jennie sitting on the
floor, in a corner, looking at the pictures in "Mother
Goose's Melodies," her dolls and toys scattered around.
Presently she got up, and went to her Father, holding
her book, and said :

"Oh, Father! see the nice new book
　　Aunt Nancy bought for me ;
Now take it in your hand and look,
　　'Tis Mother Goose, you see.
Here is a picture of her, too,
　　Her funny face and cap,
Just as she looked I know to you ;
　　So take me in your lap,
And tell me all about her now—
　　What were her children's names ?
Where did she live ?　I want to know
　　About their merry games."

34

"MY DEAR, I AM SURPRISED TO SEE SUCH IGNORANCE IN ONE SO OLD."

HOUSE ON THE HILL. Page 35.

FATHER.

(Laying down his book, and speaking pompously).
My dear, I am surprised to see
    Such ignorance in one so old ;
In eight months more, *six years* you'll be,
    And yet this fact must now be told,
No ancient lady by the name
    Of Mother Goose, was ever seen.
'Tis but a fable ; all the same
    As many other tales have been.
I'll buy for you a nice new book
    I see has just come out,
A work on Physiology,
    By Nicodemus Grout.

JENNIE.
Oh, Pa ! I'm sorry it is so,
    I loved the dear old Dame ;
But back to Dolly I will go,
    From Santa Claus that came.

35

FATHER.

From Santa Claus ?   O foolish child !
   Never again believe in him ;
'Tis but a fancy, vain and wild —
   To trust in him I fear is sin.

JENNIE.

(Goes away looking very sad.)

Oh, dear, how sorry I do seem—
   I'll put my Doll to bed ;
I don't know what the 'olgies mean—
   Poor Santa Claus is dead !

PAUL.

*(Comes into the room with bow and arrow in his hand.   Goes
to Jennie.)*

What's the matter, little sis ?
Why are you so sad as this ?

See my arrow, see my bow —
This is the way I make them go.

> (*Points his bow and arrow at her.*)

I am William Tell, you see,
You his little boy shall be.
Put this apple on your head—
Hit it I, or you'll be dead.

FATHER.

> (*Looks up in an absent way.*)

William Tell?—my son, did I just hear you mention
That gentleman's name?   Then, for your information,
You'll allow me to read, from this paper I hold,
A fact just discovered, but still very old.
It is all a mistake that he ever existed,
Or at least in the battle for freedom enlisted.
'Tis certain he never was Swissman at all,
For the story's almost as old as the Fall.

37

Paul.

(*Thinking a minute.*)

Well, then, Indians we will be,
Living in the woods so free;
Philip *I*, with lordly air,
You, the Pocahontas fair!

Father.

Alas, my son! I'm sorry now to say,
That History still is far out of the way.

Paul.

(*Interrupts him.*)

I'll not believe a word he says—
The tiresome, peeking, prying man!
How should *he* ever know, I pray,
What's happened since the world began!

He'll never do one half the good
That dear old Mother Goose has done ;
He should be hung out in the wood,
For spoiling all our play and fun.
(*Paul goes out in a passion, and calls Jennie to go with him.*)

FATHER.

"To be sure there is some truth in what the lad says. It is hard to break up old associations. But this is a *progressive age*, and a change must be made in the mode of educating children. Some more solid and substantial works should take the place of Robinson Crusoe, and other tales. Müller's Science of Language would not be amiss, if it were abridged.

"Some good Chemical work, too, and lectures on Geology and Mineralogy, are needed.

"History, ancient and modern, must be re-written. I must give this matter my serious attention.

(*Rises and walks about the room.*)

39

"Perhaps Agassiz might be induced to prepare a new book for children, from five to seven, on some scientific subject. Then there is Ruskin—a treatise upon Greek and Roman art would be just the thing for boys of ten years of age.

"If some of our literary men will take up the subject, we can gain at least ten years in the life of a child; in fact, I think that by proper and judicious training, we may, in time, entirely dispense with Childhood."

Much laughter and applause followed the little Dialogue.

"Oh, no," said Mamma; "do not let us try to put 'old heads on the dear little shoulders,' or fill them with ideas they cannot understand. Time enough for that. There is nothing so sad, as an *old* little child. Rather would I prolong their childhood. I have no patience with the 'March of Intellect,' when it marches through the ranks of Childhood. But this is too serious. Now for the Christmas Tree!"

And she threw open the folding-doors. There it stood, one blaze of light, loaded with wonderful fruit. Hand in hand, the children formed a circle round it, silent with admiration and happiness. Every branch bore a gift for some one of the happy circle, and even the green moss in which it stood was covered with packages, too bulky for the slender limbs.

Not one was forgotten; even the servants, who had come in to see the beautiful Tree, were remembered; and very strangely, the children thought, Santa Claus had given every one just what they most wanted.

They looked and talked, and played with and admired the new gifts, till one by one the little wax tapers burned away, and the Tree stood alone, all its fruit gathered, and nothing but bits of red, white and blue wax scattered over its dark green leaves.

"I wish it could always be green and fresh," said Jennie. "I do not like to have it wither and dry up, and at last be burned, like any common tree."

"Look here, my little girl," said Papa, and he lifted the moss, and showed her the long roots of the tree. "See, I have had it taken up with all its roots, so that we can plant it in the garden ; and I hope it will live and flourish many years!"

"And," said the Mother, "it will always remind us of this happy Christmas Day. Come with me to the piano, and we will sing our little Christmas Hymn, and then we will say good-night."

So, standing around her, as she played, the children joined their clear voices in singing together Mamma's

CHRISTMAS HYMN.

Sing, children, sing,
Sing a merry Christmas lay,
Jesus Christ was born to-day—
He, the Life, the Truth, the Way!
Sing, children, sing!

Look, children, look,
See o'er Syria's plains afar,
How that brightly beaming star,
Shines where Babe and Mother are!
Look, children, look!

Hark, children, hark!
Do you hear the angels sing—
"List the tiding that we bring,
Christ is born, your God, your King!"
Hark, children, hark!

Pray, children, pray,
Christ the Saviour lives on high,
But He hears the humblest cry!—
Ever loving, ever nigh.
Pray, children, pray!

THE CROSS OLD MAN.

NCE there was a man who lived in an old, old house ; but it was a very good house, and everything was pleasant around it, and this man had many things to make him happy. But he was *not* happy. He was always grumbling, grumbling. He used to sit down every night by the fire in the kitchen, and fret, and scold, and grumble, and say, "What a miserable man I am."

Now, there was an old Cricket lived in a corner of the big fire-place. He had lived there a great many years, and brought up a large family of children, and taught them all to be merry and good. And though he

44

"HE TOOK THE POKER AND POKED IT INTO ALL THE HOLES IN THE
HEARTH."

was an old Grandpa Cricket, that often had the asthma, and was always troubled with rheumatism, yet he was always cheerful, and never had the *blues*, but sat on a brick, in the warm corner, and sang every evening.

Well, this cross man could not bear to hear the Cricket sing, for he thought he said : " *Don't you fret, don't you fret—try to be happy, try to be happy.*"

So the man—the cross man, hated the poor old Cricket, and he took the poker and poked it into all the holes in the hearth, and among the bricks in the old chimney, to try and kill the Cricket.

But he could not find him. Then he sent for a mason with a big hod of mortar, and a whole load of bricks, and told him to make a new hearth, and be *sure* to kill the Cricket if he found him.

Ah, Mr. Mason! you need not look. The Cricket is safe half way up the old fire-place, watching you from his little corner. But he is as black as the old smoky bricks, and you cannot see him.

45

And the next night he sang louder than ever. Then the cross man said : " I won't live here any longer." So, the following morning, he packed up all his boxes, and all his trunks, and away he went to another house.

Now, this new house was by the side of a river, and there was not a Cricket in the house. So, when it came night, the old man sat down by the fire, with his pipe, to have a good time grumbling, with nothing to disturb him.

He had just begun to smoke, and to think what an unhappy man he was, and how everything was going wrong, when he heard *such* a noise out at the door, and on the bank of the river. First, he could hear a great hoarse voice saying : " *Are you there? are you there?*" And then another : " *Stop your grumbling, stop your grumbling!*"

The poor man jumped up and ran to the door, and made a great shouting, to frighten the frogs away, for it was the frogs — the big frogs and the little frogs — that were making such a noise. But it did not do a bit of good. They only croaked the louder, "*Stop your grumbling! stop your grumbling!*"

And when he went by the daylight to find them, they hid in the long grass, or hopped into the water.

So, once more he packed up his boxes and trunks, and went to live in another spot, by the side of a wood, with no water near, and no fire-places—nothing but stoves in the house.

And that night he smoked and fretted in peace, and sat up an hour longer, to make up for lost time.

And when he pulled his night-cap over his ears, and tucked himself up in bed, he was in a state of perfect misery, and thought, in all the world there was not such another unhappy man.

Well, he had just got asleep, and was dreaming over his troubles, when he heard a terrible noise close to the window. Something seemed to say: "*Who are you-o-o-o? who are you-o-o-o?*" and then he saw two great staring eyes looking in at the window.

47

All he could do, he could not stop that doleful hooting. He put his head out the window, though he knew he would take a dreadful cold, and tried to drive away the ugly owl. But he only went to the next tree and began again: "I know you-o-o-o! I know you-o-o-o! to-whit-to-whoo; to-whit-to-whoo!"

The next day the cross man bought a gun, and went all over the woods, to shoot the owl. It was of no use. He could not find him in the day-time, though he came every night to sit on the tree and hoot.

So, the old man packed up his boxes and trunks once more, and went off to find another house.

This time he chose one in the middle of the town, in a crowded street; a new house—not a hole where a cricket could hide, nor a tree near for an owl, nor a bit of water or grass to be seen.

Certainly he could sleep in peace here. He went to bed early, and got to sleep, and had a beautiful dream —how he lost all his money, and I don't know what trouble beside (the worse the dream, the more he enjoyed it).

But just as he was in the pleasantest part of it, he was awakened by the bells ringing, and the engines rattling by, and the people screaming : " *Fire! fire!*"

He did not get up, for the fire was not near ; and just as he was going off to sleep again, back came the engines, rattling along, and woke him once more.

There were six fires that night, and every time he woke up ; and, at last, just at daylight, when he was having a charming nap :—

> Ding, ding, ding ! the old milkman's bell ;
> And toot, toot, toot ! fresh fish to sell.

And then the little news-boys, with the *Tribune-ne-ne*, *Times*, *World*, and *Herald-ee-ee*, screaming at the top of their voices.

Poor old man ! he jumped out of bed in perfect

49

despair. "This is worse than all the rest," said he, as he was trying to dress himself in the cold morning. And then he thought—yes, the cross old man thought, how he had run away from a little trouble, and found a worse one in every place.

"I'll go right back to the old house," he said, "and leave off my grumbling."

So he went back with all his trunks and all his boxes, and by-and-by the cross man grew pleasant and kind, and everybody liked him. He and the old Cricket became excellent friends, and used to whistle and sing together every night, beside the warm kitchen fire in the big fire-place of the Old House.

DO YOU KNOW?

ITTLE children, do you know,
  Where the little birds all go,
  When the winter wind blows cold,
  When the summer days are told?

Little children, can you tell,
  Where the ants and crickets dwell?
  Where the flowers and grasses hide,
  While the snow is drifting wide?

Little children, do you think,
  When the western sun does sink,

51

Who will keep you in the night,
Through the darkness till the light?

Little children, do not fear,
God, the God of love, is near;
And around your bed will keep
Holy angels, while you sleep.

He will guide the birdling's wing,
Food unto the raven bring;
Keep each bug, and bird and flower,
Through the dreary winter hour;

Hear the little children's prayer,
Watch them with His loving care,
And wherever they may be,
Say, "Dear children, come to Me!"

THE BLACK MARK.

A Fairy Story for Alice.

HERE was once a little girl whose name was Maud; she was very pretty, and her Papa and Mamma loved her dearly, and bought a great many toys and beautiful things to make her happy.

She had one little brother named Henri.

Once when Maud was a very little baby, her Mother was rocking her, and singing little hymns to her. She looked at her baby's sweet face, and wished it could always be so pleasant. She hoped she would be a good little girl. She wished she could keep her from ever being naughty.

53

While she was thinking about it, she heard the door open, and, looking round, she saw an old, old woman come into the room. She had on a red cloak, and a white cap, and a queer, pointed hood on her head.

In her hand she carried a little wooden pail full of black paint, and a brush was standing in it. In the other hand she held a cane, with a big yellow ball on the top of it.

She hobbled across the floor, and came and looked at the baby.

"That's a nice baby," she said. "I am the Fairy Crossette; I go round to visit all the little children, and when I find any of them naughty, I steal up behind them, and make a great *black mark* on their faces with my brush. And there the mark must stay till they have done some good and kind action. *Then*, my sister Pleasantette will wipe it away with a white cloth."

Then she put her hand in her big pocket, and took

54

"I WANT IT ALL; AND SHE TRIED TO PULL IT FROM HER PAPA'S HAND."

HOUSE ON THE HILL.   Page 55.

out a little ring, which she told Maude's Mother to put on the baby's finger, so that she might remember.

Well, little Maud grew very fast, and her Mamma took such nice care of her that she never did anything but laugh and play, and did not get any black marks on her pretty face until she was a big girl.

I will tell you how the first one happened to come.

Her Papa brought home one day a nice basket of fruit and candies. He divided them equally between Maud and little Henri. But there was only *one* large golden pear. Now, when Maud saw the pear, she wanted it very much. And when her Papa said :

"I will cut the pear, and Maud shall have half and Henri half;" Maud was not willing, and she said : "No; give *me* the pear. I want it all;" and she tried to pull it from her Papa's hand. And she grew very angry when he would not give it to her. All of a sudden she felt something on her face ; her eyes and cheeks felt strangely, and as she looked round, she saw the old Fairy Crossette just going out the door. She knew it was her brush she had felt on her face, and that there was a great *black mark* there.

She put both hands over her face, so no one could see it, and then ran fast away.

She was very much frightened. She tried to wash the mark away. She rubbed it a long time very hard, with a cloth, but it did no good.

She ran out in the garden, hoping the fresh air would drive it away. But there it stayed, looking blacker and blacker.

"Oh, dear, dear," said little Maud. "What shall I do?" When she went in to dinner, every one said:

"What has happened to Maud? How bad her face looks." But her Mamma looked sad, for she knew the old Fairy Crossette had been there. Then she called Maud to her, and said:

"Oh, poor little girl, I am sorry you have been so naughty!" She held her up to the glass, and let her see how her face looked. And she told Maud it would never be pretty again till she was a good girl, and did something pleasant and kind.

But Maud did not feel pleasant. She did not want her face to be black, yet she did not try to be good. She went wandering about by herself, for she did not like to hear people say :

"How bad Maud looks!"

By-and-by Papa took little Henri out to ride with Mamma, but he said, "Maud cannot go. I would not like any one to see that black face." So they left her at home alone. Then, when she was all alone, she thought how naughty she had been, and was very sorry. She wished Henri would come, so that she could tell him how sorry she was, and ask her Papa to forgive her. And she said :

"I will kiss Henri, and give him the sugar-cow and man Mamma gave me, and I will ask Papa to give him all the pear." So she got the cow and man, and sat down to watch for them, in her little chair at the window. At last she saw them coming home. She ran to meet them. "I am sorry I was bad to you little brother," she said ; "but you may have *all* the pear, and here is a cow and a man for you."

Then, as she stooped down to kiss Henri, she felt something very soft pass over her face, and she knew it was the good Fairy Pleasantette wiping away the black mark. And when she looked up, her Papa said :

"Ah, my little Maud's sweet face has come back again ;" and he kissed her, and her Mamma was very happy, too, and hoped her face would never get marked again by the old fairy.

It did not for a long time, and it never again stayed black so long. For Maud would look at her little ring, and think quickly, and try to be good. and, by-and-by, her face did not get marked at all.

So old Crossette would come, and look grumbling in at the door, and say : "It is of no use to come here,

Maud is always trying to be good now. I must go elsewhere to find boys and girls to mark."

Well, so she goes hobbling all over the world, with the help of her cane, and when she sees a little child cross and unkind, or selfish, or disobedient, she puts a great black mark on its face.

But then the good little Fairy Pleasantette follows after her, and as soon as the little children are sorry, and try to be good, she takes out her nice little white napkin and wipes away the ugly *Black Mark*.

THE SEARCH FOR FAIRY LAND;

OR,

A DAY IN THE WOODS.

NE bright morning two little children walked hand in hand along a green lane. They were going to spend the day on the hill, and in the woods.

They thought they could see in the distance a spot so beautiful that it must be Fairy Land.

It was a little valley between two high hills. A brook ran dancing along over mossy stones, sometimes leaping a long way over a high bank, and then quietly moving along in the bright sunshine, or through the shady grove, until, with one great bound, it fell into the broad river that flowed at the foot of the hill.

A little grove of low pines and spruces sheltered it. Higher up, on the top of the hill, was a thick forest. There the children did not wish to go. It looked so dark, and the wind roared so loudly through the thick branches of the trees. They thought there must be bears there, and, perhaps, lions and tigers. No, they would never go into the dark forest.

But the pleasant little valley, with its wood of pines — had they not sat on the steps of the piazza, many a time, and watched the shadows move swiftly over the tree-tops and along the soft grass, and seen the little brook glistening in the sunbeams as it ran frolicking among the trees? And only the night before, they had asked their Mother to let them go and stay all day on the hill.

Pleasant were their dreams that night. Bertie thought he was a squirrel, bounding from tree to tree; and Grace dreamed that she was sleeping on a mossy bank, and a little bird came and sang in her ear:

" Come, little Gracie, come with me,
And see my nest in the old, old tree !"

and just as she was jumping up to go, Bertie threw a
whole handful of rose leaves in her face, and frightened
the bird away.   She awoke, and found part of her
dream was true ; for there *was* Bertie with his hands
full of roses, calling " Gracie, Gracie ! wake up.   Breakfast is ready ; and our Mother says if we *should* find
the fairies, they would give us nothing but dew-drops
to eat.   So we shall want our breakfast, and the nice
little basket of lunch she has packed for us."

Grace was soon ready, their breakfast quickly eaten,
and the good-bye kiss given to their Mother, who charged
them not to wander too far, and so they set out on their
journey.

" We are like Christian in 'The Pilgrim's Progress,'
said Bertie ; " we are going to climb the Hill of Diffi-
culty."

"No," said Grace. "I don't think it will be very difficult. It is not very steep, and see how many nice rocks there are to rest upon."

So, on, on they went — now stopping to rest, and often gathering the wild flowers and pretty mosses.

"Look! there is our Mother," said Bertie (for they were so high they could look down upon their own home)—"see! she has a basket in her hand. She is going into the garden. What do you think she is going to do, Grace?"

"I don't know — pick strawberries, I think. Oh, there is Father, too! he has got old Jim. He is going to ride."

"So he is," said Bertie. "I wish I were going too."

"But you had rather go with me in the woods, Bertie. Come, do not let us sit here any longer. The sun is hot, and I want to go into the cool shade."

So they ran along, jumping from one mound of moss to another, till they began to descend into the little valley. Soon they were standing by the side of the brook.

They walked slowly along, looking into its clear waters, and watching the little waves dash against the stones, and then flow round, or over them, making a white foam, or tiny whirlpool.

At last they reached the pleasant spot, among the trees, they had so often longed to visit. And lovely it was indeed. A circle of soft grass and mound of moss, enclosed on every side by low pines — the pretty brook falling over a little pile of stones, and then widening into a miniature pond. The water so clear that every pebble could be seen, and every leaf or tiny fish.

Gracie clapped her hands and danced about.

" Oh, is it not beautiful, Bertie ! I can see our home far away at the foot of the hill ; and I can see the river, too, and the church. Let us take off our shoes and stockings and wade in the brook."

" So we will," said Bertie. " I want to get some of those shining pebbles at the bottom of the brook."

So they took off their shoes and stockings, and waded

all about in the cool, clear water, and Bertie got whole handsful of bright stones, and laid them on the bank to dry.

" I do believe some of them are gold," said he ; " and these white ones are certainly crystal."

Then they picked the green leaves, and sailed them down the brook for boats. On one large leaf Bertie placed a grasshopper, that sat very contentedly, and seemed to enjoy his sail, till the leaf went against a large stone in the middle of the brook. The grass-hopper jumped off upon the stone, and the leaf went sailing on.

" Oh, he is Robinson Crusoe on the desert island ! He must have a man Friday to live with him," said Grace.

She soon found a little black beetle, which she sent sailing after him. But the man Friday did not fancy the frail boat, and soon crawled off into the water. There he threw out his black legs and sprawled about, till Bertie caught him on the end of a long stick, and landed him safely on the island. However, Grass-hopper Crusoe did not give him a warm welcome; he seemed perfectly content to dwell alone, and sat in dignified silence, until Friday the beetle explored the island. He soon found a cave large enough to hold him, when he crawled away out of sight.

"Good-bye, poor old Robinson Crusoe!" said Bertie. "We will come and make you a call before we go home."

"We will not eat our dinner yet," said Grace, "and I do not need this large shawl; let us hang it over these low trees for a tent. It shall be our house. We will have this large flat stone for our table. I willll spread leaves over it, and put our basket of lunch on it, so that it will be all ready. Now, Bertie, let us play that we are going a hunting."

"Yes," said Bertie; "but you ought to stay at home and keep house."

"No, indeed! I shall hunt, too. See, I have a

66

gun!" and she caught up a stick, and ran laughing up the hill. Bertie took another stick and followed.

And now what fun they had. Every nook and corner of the sunny old hill was explored.

They climbed the low trees to look into the birds' nests. They peeped in the holes under the rocks — "For, perhaps," said Grace, "they lead to Fairy Land."

"Take care an ugly Brownie does not jump out, and drag you down, down in the dark, cold ground to the cavern where they make the bright diamonds. You would not like working there quite as well as running about in this bright sunshine. So take care, sister, how you poke your head in too far."

"Oh, I wish he would!" said Grace. "I would not be afraid. I do so long to see one of those queer little people. They could not keep me. I should soon come back to you with my hands full of diamonds."

"Oh, thank you! I have plenty of diamonds from the bottom of the brook. But look, sister, there is a hole

that does really look as if it might lead somewhere.
See the long winding tunnel, now over, now round the
mossy bank. There is certainly a Brownie at the end
of it—a blind Brownie, too—for, Grace, a little mole
made the road. The gardener told me all about it.
He has been setting traps on the lawn to catch them,
for he says they destroy the roots of the grass, and do
a great deal of harm."

"Oh, Bertie! do you mean the pretty little creature
that Fred had caught, and that you brought in to show
me? He had such soft fur, and queer little feet, and
long nose. Did he really make such a long tunnel as
this? Do you suppose his house is at the end of it?

"Yes, indeed! and perhaps a whole family of them.
They are very troublesome, and ought to be extermin-
ated," said Bertie, bringing out one of the gardener's
long words with a great flourish.

But just then they spied something that put the moles,
and Brownies, and everything else, out of their minds.

"FOR A MINUTE THEY LAY AND LOOKED, TOO FRIGHTENED TO
RECOGNIZE THE LAUGHING EYES AND ROSY CHEEKS."

HOUSE ON THE HILL.   Page 68.

Strawberries — yes, just below them was a spot of ground so thickly covered, that it looked red with them. Large, too, and sweet and delicious, as only the wild mountain strawberry can be.

"Stay here, Grace, and I will run for the basket. Will they not be nice with our dinner?"

In a few minutes he was back with the empty basket. It was soon filled, and they walked slowly back to their tent.

They found their dinner all safe in its white napkin, though they had had some fear that it might have been eaten, or carried away by mountain thieves, in the shape of squirrels or birds. They soon arranged it in nice order on their stone table. Bertie brought water from the brook in a little tin mug his Mother had placed in the basket. Grace folded leaves into baskets, to hold their strawberries, and strewed wild flowers among them.

They both agreed as they sat talking, laughing and

eating, that it was the nicest dinner they had ever eaten, and that they would like to live in the woods all the time — only in the winter, when the snow was on the ground, and the cold wind whistled among the trees — then they would rather be safe at home.

"Look, Bertie, quick, in that old tree, there is a squirrel peeping at us! I do believe he wants some of our dinner!"

"Oh, Grace!" said her brother; "I have thought of *such* a plan — how we can get all the squirrels and birds, and, perhaps, the Fairies and Brownies, too, to come and dine with us.

"Let us lay all these pieces of bread, and cake, and cold meat, on the ground, where they can see them; and then you and I will lie down on this mossy bank and cover ourselves with leaves, so that they cannot see us. We will leave a place for our eyes to peep out, and watch what they will do."

"So we will," said Grace; and she began to strew

the crumbs around, while Bertie gathered whole handfuls of leaves and small branches of trees.

Then they both lay down, and Bertie covered Grace and himself with leaves, only leaving their bright little eyes to watch.

They lay very still a long time, only speaking to one another in whispers. Grace was just beginning to grow sleepy, when they heard a little noise—a little pattering noise, like tiny feet stepping over the leaves.

In a minute the head and bright eyes of a squirrel, were seen peeping around the trunk of a small tree. He turned his head in every direction; now up, now down, to make sure there was no concealed enemy near.

He did not see the little "Babes in the Woods," covered over with leaves. He might have thought the four bright eyes that were watching him, were only the bright spots on some gay butterfly's wing. They were not enemies, though Bunny would have ran very quickly

71

back to his hole had he seen them. But he seemed satisfied there was no danger, for he came down on the ground and began nibbling a bit of bread. Presently he stopped eating, and made a little sound, raising his head and looking back to the tree.

"What can he be doing?" whispered Grace.

"Hush, hush!" said Bertie; "don't you see he is calling his children. Oh, look! see them all coming!"

And sure enough they were coming. Five little squirrels, with nice bushy tails, came bounding along — for they knew there was no danger when their mother called them — and in a minute after a larger squirrel came slowly after them. It was the old papa squirrel, who had been out hunting for nuts, and just come home with two nice ones for his children, to find them all gone from home.

But he soon found them, and came to help them eat the nice bread and cake; and as he was a good, saving papa, he filled both cheeks with bread to carry home to their nest for another day.

Seven squirrels in all, quite a dinner party — but soon more guests arrived; for the birds, seeing how nicely the squirrels were faring, thought they too would come. There were two old robins, with their little son Bobby; there were yellow birds, and blue birds, and brown birds, and a bright, red-headed woodpecker, who had been poking his long bill into little holes in the trees, searching for grubs and insects.

They all hopped about, chattering and talking to one another, bird-fashion, and picking up the crumbs and strawberries that were left.

What fun they had, and what a merry company! Bertie and Grace could hardly lie still, they were so pleased and excited; and when a little brown rabbit came running out of the bushes, Grace did say, " Oh," so loud as to make them all jump and turn their little heads, and flutter their wings, as if they would all run away; but as they did not hear another sound, they soon began their dinner again.

And now I wish you could have seen, as Bertie and Grace saw, how cunning these little creatures were. The old squirrel got up on the table and nibbled the bread into little bits, and then he would give it to his children, and cuff their ears if they were greedy, or tried to pull it one from the other; and they kept up such a chattering, too, and ran around and whisked their long tails, and looked sideways at the old rabbit, who had come alone, and sat in a corner holding a bit of cake in his fore-paws, and nibbling it in a very dignified manner.

And then the birds—they flew about and made such a noise. They were too busy eating, or they would have noticed how many little bugs, and ants and crickets, had come to the party, and were helping themselves to the nicest bits. But the children saw them, and re-joiced in the company they had collected together. They only wished they might come out from their hiding place and join them.

"Oh, Bertie, what fun this is! How I wish the Fairies and Brownies would come too!"

"Perhaps they will," said Bertie. "Oh, Grace, look between those two trees! There is a face peeping between the leaves. Who can it be?"

For a minute they lay and looked, too frightened to recognize the laughing eyes and rosy cheeks. They certainly thought it must be one of the little folks they had been talking about.

So, forgetting that they had wished them to come, they sprang up to run away. Oh, the poor birds and squirrels that were so happily eating their dinner!

In a minute they were all gone, and the head of the Brownie changed suddenly to that of their own brother Robert, who jumped out of the bushes quite as much astonished as they.

"Why, Grace and Herbert, are you here? I heard a great chattering as I was looking for you, and crept softly through the bushes to see what it was. I have been watching those little creatures a long time, but I did not think *you* were here. You seemed to rise up out of the ground!"

"Yes," said Bertie; "do you not see how nicely we hid ourselves?" And then he told Robert what they had done, and how much fun they had had, and how they thought he was a Brownie, and were so surprised they forgot to lie still, and so frightened their company that it all ran away.

Robert laughed heartily at their mistake, but said he thought it was an excellent plan, and he meant to try it himself sometime.

"But now," said he, "you must go home. Mother sent me to find you."

"Well," said Bertie, "but first let me get my beautiful pebbles." And he took the basket to bring them.

"Oh, Robert, they are so bright. I will give you some to put in your cabinet!"

He ran to the place where he had put them to dry.

But they were gone, or, rather, they had changed to such dull, dirty colors. Robert laughed at his doleful face.

"Did you take them out of the water, little brother?"

"Yes," said Bertie.

"Well, that is why they look so dull. Throw them back, and they will soon grow bright again."

Herbert did so. "I did not know it was the water that made them bright. I thought they would always look so," said he.

"Let us go and see Robinson Crusoe," said Grace; "we told him we would come."

"Who is *he*?" said Robert.

"A big grasshopper we put on a stone in the middle of the brook. Come and see him."

But he was gone. What became of him—whether a vessel came and took him off—or he swam to the mainland—or was drowned in the attempt, they never knew. He and his man Friday had both disappeared.

"Gone certainly," said Robert. "Now 'follow your

leader' home ;" and away he ran, the children bounding after him.

On the high rocks, down in the low glens among the trees and bushes, he led them, till they saw him at last standing on a log running out into the river, and there they were afraid to follow him.

The rest of the way was a quiet walk by the water side, and the sun was just setting, when the tired, but happy children, reached home, well pleased with their pleasant " Day in the Woods."

THE END.

www.ingramcontent.com/pod-product-compliance
Lightning Source LLC
Chambersburg PA
CBHW031445270326
41930CB00007B/879